**Consultant** Sue Barber
**Photography** © Fiona Pragoff
**Illustrations** Colin Mier
**Additional Design** Amanda McCourt

Copyright © Two-Can Publishing Ltd, 1996

This edition published in 1996 by
Two-Can Publishing Ltd, 346 Old Street, London EC1V 9NQ
in association with
Watts Books, 96 Leonard Street, London EC2A 4RH

Printed and bound by Wing King Tong (Hong Kong)

2 4 6 8 10 9 7 5 3 1

All rights reserved. No part of this publication may be reproduced, stored in a retrieval system
or transmitted in any form or by any means electronic, mechanical, photocopying, recording
or otherwise, without prior written permission of the copyright owner.

A catalogue record for this book is available from the British Library

ISBN 1-85434-350-5 (hardback)
ISBN 1-85434-351-3 (paperback)

# CONTENTS

I WANT TO BE . . . 4

LETTING GO . . . 6

HAPPY OR SAD? . . . 8

BODY LANGUAGE . . . 10

ACT IT OUT . . . 12

QUICK CHANGE! . . . 14

PICK A THEME . . . 16

LOOK THE PART . . . 18

TELL A STORY . . . 20

FACE CHANGE . . . 22

BITS AND PIECES . . . 24

SET THE SCENE . . . 26

GETTING READY . . . 28

PUTTING ON A SHOW . . . 30

# I WANT TO BE AN ACTOR

Putting on a play involves all sorts of different skills and it's good to know as much as possible about all the different jobs involved. There are costumes to make, props and scenery to get ready and make-up to apply. And, of course, there are all the acting techniques to learn, too! Acting may be hard work, but it's also good fun and you'll make lots of friends.

Painting scenery and backdrops is just one of the jobs involved in putting on a play

Dressing up will help you get into the character of the person you are playing

# LETTING GO

Actors need to be as relaxed as possible. If they are tense they may make mistakes! And they need to be fit, too. Acting is a tough job!

### Warming up
Before taking part in a play, or rehearsing, actors do exercises to loosen up their bodies and voices. Breathing exercises are useful, too. Stand up straight and take slow, deep breaths. Feel your lungs fill with air.

### Ooooh, aaaahhhh!
Try some voice exercises to help loosen up. Look in a mirror and make a yawning noise. Alter the shape of your mouth and use your lips and tongue. Practise singing, shouting and whispering.

Use a mirror so you can see the shape of your mouth when you make different sounds

Don't worry if you look daft, actors often have to do peculiar things!

# HAPPY OR SAD?

Now it's time to start acting! Let's start with faces and expresssions. Look at the people around you. Can you tell from their faces what they are thinking or feeling?

Happy

**Showing how you feel**
In real life, people don't think about showing their feelings.

**Face up to it!**
Your face is a very useful tool. You can use your eyes, nose and mouth to show different emotions or feelings.

Sad

Puzzled

When you're sad you may burst into tears and when someone tells a joke you'll probably laugh. On stage you'll have to switch feelings on and off, no matter how you really feel.

Try some of these in front of a mirror – raise your eyebrows, wrinkle your nose, open your mouth, make your eyes into narrow slits.

**People watch!**
When you are out and about look for people showing their feelings. They may be angry, sad, impatient or bored.

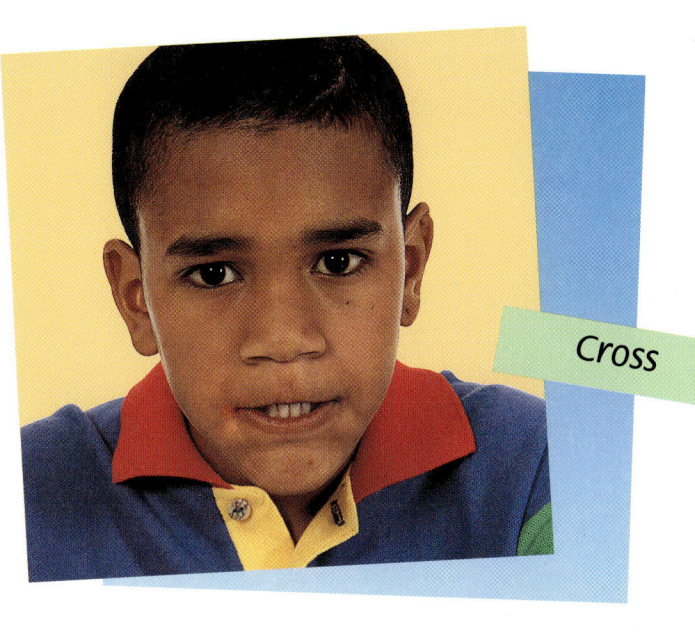

Cross

As soon as you get a chance, try imitating them in front of a mirror.

Scared

Looking terrified is easy. I just have to think about slugs and snails!

# BODY LANGUAGE

Your face can tell a lot about how you feel, but so can the rest of your body! You can 'say' a lot using body language without speaking at all! Actors need to use body language all the time.

## Walking tall?

A confident, happy person will walk with their head up. They will not be afraid to meet your eye and might nod or raise a friendly hand. A shy person is more likely to walk with their head down and will avoid catching your eye.

If I've told you once, I've told you 5 million times

I hope everyone is convinced by my acting!

How am I going to get out of this one?

Chin sticking out, finger pointed and shaking

Eyes wide open in fear. Hand to mouth to cover up confusion

Both people are making it very clear how they feel by their actions

# ACT IT OUT

Here are some great exercises to try with your friends. They will help get your imagination running wild and give you practise in working with space!

**What's in the box?**
Sit in a circle with some friends and pass round an empty box. Take it in turns to take something out of the box and describe it. No words allowed!

Worms have a funny effect on people! How would you pretend to take one out of a box?

Acting without words is known as miming. You'll probably find it quite difficult to begin with, but keep practising and it will become easy! Use big, bold gestures with your hands and arms and make your face work hard, too.

**Walk About**
When you are on a stage with other people you will have to know where they are all the time. Learning to share a small space with others is very important. Practise this with some friends. Walk around a room without bumping into anyone – look for the spaces and walk towards them.

*That was a close shave. I nearly bumped into him!*

*Use this exercise to practise different ways of walking*

*Pleased to feet you!*

**How do you do!**
Now try walking around the room with your eyes focussed on just one other person. Don't lose sight of them but don't walk close to them either. And try not to bump into anyone! Finally, walk around and greet each person you meet in a different way. Use a different voice, change the greeting, use new actions. Be as mad as you like!

# QUICK CHANGE!

You are probably thinking about putting on a play by now! But before you start making costumes and gathering props together try some instant dressing up.

*Be careful when you sit down!*

### Instant stuffing!
Tie a pillow or cushion round your tummy. Now put on some oversize clothes. Hey presto, you are very fat!

*Visit the kitchen and turn into a daring knight in armour!*

*Wooden spoon sword*

*Colander for a helmet*

*Protect yourself with a saucepan lid shield*

*Paint hair and eyebrows on bag*

*Paint face with green face paint!*

### Monster madness
An ordinary brown paper bag can turn you into a scary Frankenstein monster in a matter of minutes.

## Two in one
How many different characters can you turn yourself into with just one scarf, or large square of fabric?

A pirate?

Or a bank robber?

## Up, up and away!
Find the right hat, add a pair of swimming goggles and you are an old-fashioned pilot!

It's a bit chilly up here above the clouds

Mmmm! Those drinks look good!

Or an Arab in the desert!

I'd rather be a pilot!

## Can I help?
Tie an apron around you, fold a drying-up cloth over your arm and you have become a waiter. Add a tray and some glasses and look for some thirsty customers!

15

# PICK A THEME

You've exercised your voice and your body and your imagination is running wild. Let's put on an instant show!

### Pick a theme!
We chose the seaside as the theme for our instant show. But there are plenty of other ideas! You could choose a windy day, or a circus or a camping expedition.

### In the mood!
Get together with your friends and talk about a day by the sea. What will the weather be like? What will you wear? What will you take with you? Will you have a good time? Try to smell the sea and hear the waves!

*Last time I made sand castles a daft dog dug them all up!*

Leap high in the air to catch an imaginary beach ball

Pretend to make a sandcastle. Fill the bucket, turn it upside down and lift it off carefully

# LOOK THE PART

**Now it's time to think about costumes. Dressing as the character you are going to play will help you both look and feel the part.**

### New from old
Most costumes can be put together from existing clothes. Look for bargains in junk shops and jumble sales.

### Keep a collection
Accessories, such as hats, belts, bags, scarves, ties and jewellery are all useful. Keep a look-out for old glasses without lenses. Scraps of fabric, lengths of ribbon and odd buttons may well come in handy. It pays to be a hoarder, but try to keep your collection in some sort of order so that you can find things easily!

*Tie over shoulder adds to the dishevelled look*

*I can't understand why everything looks upside down!*

*Stick cotton wool balls inside the rim of an old hat to make an instant wig for an old lady*

*Look in magazines and newspapers for inspiration!*

*An old school blazer is great for an absent minded professor*

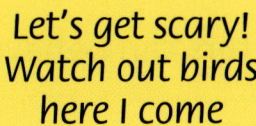
*Let's get scary! Watch out birds here I come*

## Who's in charge?

If you are putting on a play with a large cast, it's a good idea to have someone in charge of the 'wardrobe'. They can help actors who may need to change costumes quickly and might grab the wrong thing by mistake.

Real scarecrows have a pole holding them up. You'll have to pretend!

This oversize raincoat was yet another junk shop bargain

Try your local pet shop for a supply of straw!

You may have some things – like dungarees – in your wardrobe

# TIPS

★ It is a good idea to sketch out costumes on paper at an early stage. Then you can see immediately which things need to be made and which can be bought!

★ Try to keep the costumes for each character separate – large cardboard boxes may help!

# TELL A STORY

Before you embark on a full-length play, try acting out some short scenes. You could use an existing plot or make up your own storyline.

**Larger than life**
In a play the characters can behave in a totally over the top way. They don't have to behave in a normal fashion.

*I only put my bag down for a second! I was sure it would be perfectly safe*

**Who dunnit?**
We turned a simple burglary into something a bit more complicated!

*I must remember that I'm the goodie now!*

*Fast finger Freddie strikes again!*

You don't need a lot of characters. In our play, the detective doubles up as the baddie!

## Rehearsing

As soon as everyone has learned their parts you can start running through individual scenes or the whole play. These practise runs are called rehearsals. The more complicated the play the more time you'll need to rehearse.

*Can't she see I'm just a woolly ball!*

Not much happening here but she hasn't seen the spider yet!

Now she's spotted it. Look at the change in her expression and the arm movement

She's not hanging around to find out what happens next!

## Writing a script

When you have decided on your plot, you'll need to turn it into a play script. This means writing it out in speech, giving each character their own lines. You can also include some instructions for the actors to help them. Give everyone a copy so that they can learn their lines off by heart!

# FACE CHANGE

It's amazing how you can change your character instantly with a little cleverly applied make-up. Here are a few hints and tips!

### What you need
You can buy theatrical make-up in special shops but we used ordinary make-up for the characters here. A selection of brushes is useful – fat ones and thin ones!

Look out for stick-on moustaches in fancy-dress shops

### Looking older!
Start with a base coat of foundation. Choose a colour fairly close to your skin tone and put it on with a sponge – not too thick! Add wrinkles with a soft eyeshadow pencil.

Use an eyeshadow pencil to draw on a curly moustache

To find your natural wrinkles, frown, or screw your eyes up and little lines will appear! Dust talcum powder onto your hair and eyebrows to give the effect of grey hair!

22

**Be bold**

Stage make-up can be a lot stronger and more dramatic than normal make-up! To make your cheeks rosy you can add several layers of blusher over your base coat. Blend it with your finger-tips or a soft sponge. Beauty spots can be added with a soft eyeshadow pencil. Face paints come in bright, bold colours and are useful for special effects.

# TIPS

★ Work in a good light, either near a window, or you could use a lamp with a bright bulb.

★ Dress up as much as possible before you put your make-up on. This will help to prevent smudging.

Remember the pillow trick? It will add a few kilos instantly

Plenty of pink blusher on cheeks and chin for a healthy, jolly look!

For a really glamorous look, try a curly blonde wig, several coats of red lipstick and lots of eye make-up

How could anyone think I'm the baddie!

# BITS AND PIECES

**All the bits and pieces that go into making a play look as real as possible are called props – short for properties.**

### Finding props
Some props may be simple household objects which you can borrow. They may need a bit of work on them! Others will be easy enough to make.

> Draw a map on white paper, screw it up and soak it in a bowl of tea. When it dries out you'll have an ancient document

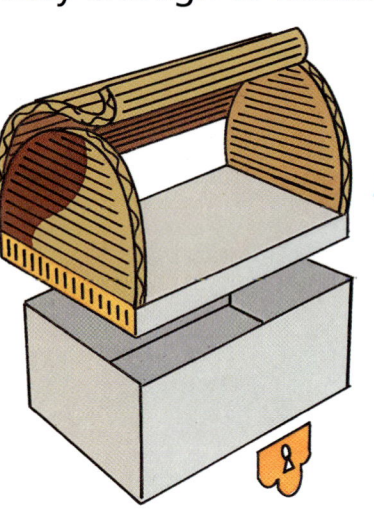

> Paint plastic glasses to make golden goblets! Use sequins and beads for jewels

> Use self-hardening clay to make jewels. Or, link paper clips to make a chain

### Pirate's treasure
Use an old shoe box as the base for your treasure chest. To make the top of the chest, cut two rounded ends from card and glue them to the lid of the shoe box. Cut a strip of thin card to fit over the ends and glue or tape it in position. The illustration on the left may help. Cut a separate lock from card and paint the box so that it looks like an old wooden chest.

**A very royal throne!**
Start with a simple kitchen chair. Make sure it won't be missed! To turn it into a throne, cut two sides and a back from thick corrugated card. You can stick the baubles on afterwards. Paint the pieces adding shields and jewels. Tape the pieces of card to the chair.

*I'm going to feel much more like the Queen when I sit on this throne*

*Measure the chair carefully before you cut out the card*

*I seem to be doing better than him!*

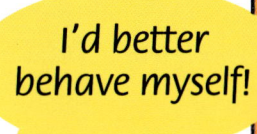
Sticks of dynamite made from cardboard tubes tied together

*I'd better behave myself!*

**Is it safe?**
Find a solid cardboard box and paint it grey to look like metal! Paint some round boxes and glue them on to the door of your safe to make a burglar proof combination lock! Larger items like the safe and throne here are often called scenery – because they help to set the scene! On the next page you'll find some more ideas.

# SET THE SCENE

**Organizing props and scenery for a play can take quite a while. Make a list of all the things you need right at the beginning of rehearsals.**

### Indoors or outdoors
Plays are often broken up into sections called acts. Each act may take place somewhere different, so you will need to change the scenery and props.

*I'm going to paint a scene behind this window so it'll look like the real thing!*

*I'd better be careful when I sit on this!*

The audience will not realise that this cleverly painted chair is actually flat!

In order to make the changes as quick as possible, it's a good idea to make scenery light and easy to move. Imagine how difficult it would be to move a heavy oak table and chairs in the few minutes you will have between acts!

## Hide and seek

Here's a great way to make a boulder that doesn't weigh a ton! Cover a cardboard box with strips of double-sided tape. Peel off the backing strips and stick on balls of scrunched up newspaper. When the box is covered you can paint the paper in shades of grey.

Leave one side of the box open to make a cave!

## Thornless cactus

Make a cactus like the one here and you definitely won't prick your finger! Cut two cactus shapes from cardboard. Make a slit from the bottom to middle of one, and from the middle to top of the other. Slot them together!

When your boulder is finished it will make a perfect hiding place!

Better hurry up, it's nearly time for the show

27

# GETTING READY

You've learned your lines, the costumes are made and the props and scenery are nearly ready. The big day is just round the corner!

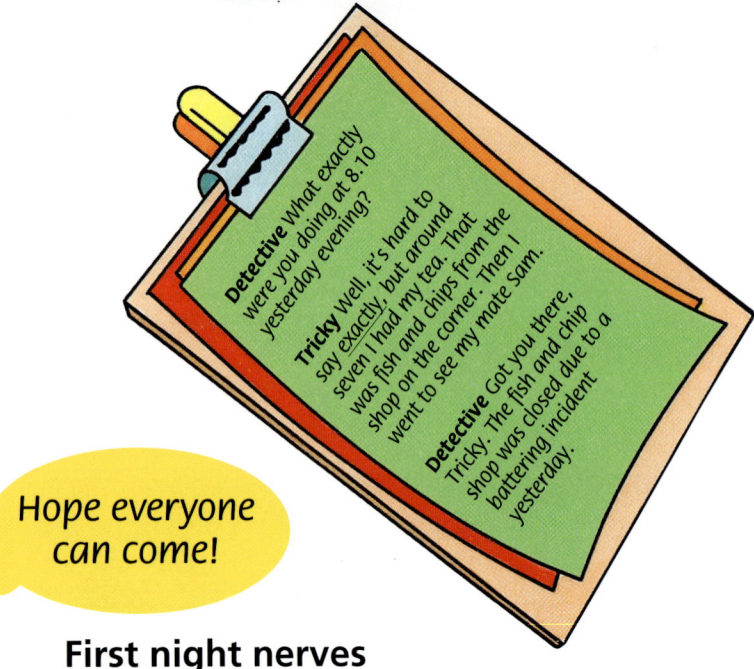

Hope everyone can come!

### First night nerves
Before you go on stage for your first show, have a final read through of your lines. Do some body stretching exercises to loosen up and some breathing exercises to help you relax.

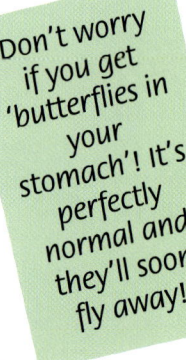

Don't worry if you get 'butterflies in your stomach'! It's perfectly normal and they'll soon fly away!

### Time and place
Make sure you have a big audience for your play. Send invitations to your friends in plenty of time and make some posters to promote the play. Don't forget to include the date, time and name of the play!

**Nearly there!**
No matter how much planning you do in advance, there are bound to be last minute panics! The backdrop may not be quite ready, or maybe the star of the show loses their voice! Make sure that you have someone who knows their part and can stand in for them at short notice!

Before the final performance have a run through with costumes, make-up and props. This is called a dress rehearsal

I hope someone has remembered the pirate ship!

I've had enough of this acting lark!

# PUTTING ON A SHOW

**The big day has arrived and it's time for the play to go ahead! Allow yourself plenty of time to put on your costume and make-up.**

### Can you hear me?
'Projecting' means being heard clearly without shouting. It's very important to practise so that everyone will be able to hear every single word – even if they are sitting at the back.

IF YOU FORGET YOUR WORDS, DON'T PANIC! COVER YOUR MISTAKE UP AS WELL AS YOU CAN AND CARRY ON AS THOUGH NOTHING HAD HAPPENED

★

NEVER EAT REAL FOOD OR DRINK ANYTHING ON STAGE. IT MAY GO DOWN THE WRONG WAY

HELP! HELP! If the crocodile doesn't get me, the pirate will

Cardboard grass surrounded by blue paper gives the impression of an island

Find out how to make the treasure chest on page 24

# INDEX

audience 5, 28
backdrops 4, 29
body language 10, 11
costumes 4, 14, 15, 18, 19, 30
dress rehearsal 29
emotions 8, 9
exercises 5, 6, 12, 13, 28
expressions 8, 9
feelings 8, 9
imagination 5, 12, 16, 17
improvising 17
invitations 28

make-up 4, 22, 23, 30
miming 12
plot 20, 21
posters 28
projecting 30
props 4, 14, 24, 25, 26, 27
rehearsal 6, 21, 26, 29
relaxing 7
scenery 4, 25, 26, 27
script 17, 21
wardrobe 19
warming up 5, 6

*The show's over! Hope you enjoyed it as much as we did!*